THE COASTAL COTTAGE

First Edition
21 20 19 18 17   5 4 3 2 1

Published by
Gibbs Smith
P.O. Box 667
Layton, Utah 84041
1.800.835.4993 orders
www.gibbs-smith.com

Designed by Sheryl Dickert
Page production by Virginia Brimhall Snow
Printed and bound in China

Gibbs Smith books are printed on either recycled, 100% post-consumer waste,
FSC-certified papers or on paper produced from sustainable PEFC-certified
forest/controlled wood source. Learn more at www.pefc.org.

Library of Congress Cataloging-in-Publication Data

Names: Zimmerman, Ann, author. | Zimmerman, Scot, photographer (expression)
Title: The coastal cottage / Ann Zimmerman ; photographs by Scot Zimmerman.
Description: Layton, Utah : Gibbs Smith, 2017.
Identifiers: LCCN 2016033796 | ISBN 9781423644125 (jacketless hardcover)
Subjects: LCSH: Cottages--United States. | Seaside architecture--United States.
Classification: LCC NA7551 .Z56 2017 | DDC 728/.370973--dc23
LC record available at https://lccn.loc.gov/2016033796

8646

THE COASTAL COTTAGE

Ann Zimmerman, photographs by Scot Zimmerman

GIBBS SMITH
TO ENRICH AND INSPIRE HUMANKIND

Contents

7 | Introduction

12 | Sailor's Life for Me

20 | Tropical Punch

32 | Polychrome Panache

44 | Living on the Edge

52 | Beachcomber's Party House

62 | Breezy and Demure

74 | Cottage for Two

82 | Quintessentially Carmel

92 | Roses and Lavender

106 | Place Remembered

116 | Set in Stone

130 | Nowhere But Up

138 | Lofty Haven

148 | Refined Comfort

164 | A Touch of the South

174 | Acknowledgments

175 | Sources

introduction

I love cottages. I love them for their modesty, charming imperfections, and whimsy. I love them for their raucous gardens, painted furniture, embroidered linens, and porch swings. To me, cottages represent living simply and beautifully.

Cottages have always been difficult to define, and this is my starting point. Especially now, with some developers calling almost-mansions cottages, there is even more confusion about what is actually meant by the term "cottage."

To me, cottages are a tradition, and the one I am most familiar with begins in England. By the 1600s, rural families built small functional homes, generally with one or two rooms below and a loft above. This time frame precedes manufacturing as well as roads and canals for commerce, and rural people built them from local materials and according to local building traditions. These "vernacular" homes, as homegrown building is called, varied substantially by region. Some were stone, others wattle and daub, some wood, some home-fired bricks, and there were numerous combinations. They were practical and efficient shelters for rural working families. In fact, the term "cottage industries" came about from the workers' side businesses in the home, like weaving, spinning, and turning chairs.

By the 1800s much had changed in England, including a rise in prosperity and proliferation of estate properties. It was popular for the wealthy to romanticize the past before industrialization. Owners regarded their estates as scenes from paintings, and they carefully sited cottages and decoratively designed them to complement the estate landscape as a picturesque ideal. This ideal, which remains today, reflected nostalgia, harmony, and a sense of natural order. A professional class of designers and builders evolved who wrote pattern books and treatises on the picturesque cottage ideal of contented cheerfulness and a balance between nature and man.

According to the pattern books, the ideal cottage includes intricacy, variety, play of outline, asymmetry, porches, overhanging eaves, recessed windows, large intricate chimneys, and gardens with creepers, shrubs, and trees. Soon, more concern grew for health, and the cottage ideal expanded to include health, warmth, comfort, and light, and pattern books expressed this by including spacious ventilated main rooms with a fireplace.

European ideals crossed the Atlantic relatively intact as the cottage concept. In the United States, proponents popularized cottages for workers as

The ideal picturesque balance was oneness between the cottage and surroundings.

practical, healthy shelters, and many of the factory and railroad cottages that were built a hundred years ago still remain. Others, including early landscape designer Andrew Jackson Downing, promoted cottage designs and pattern books for American farmhouses. (Our own cottage home is an 1880 Gothic Revival farmhouse.) The other cottage tradition, and the one that is much more familiar to all of us, is vacation homes. Cottages at the seacoast are celebrated in this book.

Of course, the influence of cottages in America continued through the twentieth century. One notable period was that featuring Arts and Crafts bungalows, and eventually cottages influenced suburban home design.

Cottages by the sea are continuing to change, and one factor is the increased rarity of buildable lots and homes in desirable coastal locations and their high costs. For example, simple cottages that not long ago were inexpensive summer homes for artists, writers, and educators in Carmel, California, now cost in the millions. Another change is climate variation and the increased severity of coastal storms. New cottage designs look to these conditions and expand and vary our modern coastal cottage traditions.

While cottages offer everything one needs, there may not be space for all that one wants. It's a balance, and there is an art to living small and well. The cottage tradition is oneness with landscape, and cottage living means expanding the living space to porches and patios outdoors.

A cottage at the beach is the perfect place for an artist to live and paint.

I asked Whidbey Island architect Ross Chapin, a cottage designer and proponent, why cottages appeal to him. "I like the simple lifestyle they offer. A good cottage is relaxed and easy, with no pretensions of impressing anyone. 'Come on in,' it says, as if through the back door, rather than asking formal introductions at the front door. Cottages might be lean on space, but every bit of space will be fully lived in. It is character that defines a cottage, not size or polished perfection. A beloved cottage enlivens the heart and celebrates relationships with family, friends, and neighbors. What's not to love about that?"

I invite you to experience coastal cottage living in the pages of this book through Scot's joyful photographs, imagining yourself in these settings and taking away design ideas for wherever you call home.

The picturesque ideal that originated over 200 years ago included porches and overhangs.

Why not let a home be a reminder of favorite seaside pastimes like sailing? With nautical colors, a porthole window, and a collection of toy ships built to scale, the pleasures of sailing will never seem too far away.

The surfboard resting at the side of the porch and the towel drying on the wooden chair tell the story of the morning's ride, just as opening the Dutch door with the porthole in the top reveals the owners' love for spending time on their boat, which is moored not too far away.

The porch is an inviting outdoor living area with its wicker rockers and a swing for two. The ceiling,

With its generous broad porch, painted board-and-batten walls, and the low angled roofline over the porch, at first glance this home resembles a simple bungalow, an early and favorite cottage design. However, the two rooflines set behind allow for living space in the top level. With the differing exterior wall finishes—natural shingles and clapboard—there is a feeling of additions over time, when in fact it is the original design.

ABOVE: The living area sets a nautical theme, and the colorful scaled toy model of a sailing vessel reinforces it.

OPPOSITE: A charming dining area is kept simple by a bare floor, painted furniture, and the ship's lantern as a hanging pendant light. The cutout on the right is a pass-through to the galley kitchen.

railings, and window frames are painted a pleasing white, which adds simplicity to the design by emphasizing the clean lines.

The Dutch door, which allows breezes through the top while keeping the dog inside, opens directly to the living area, where a comfortable sofa and rattan chairs are nestled by a wood-burning stove. The nautical theme of blue and white, dotted with playful red, appears in the artwork, the area rug accented with boats, the cabinet enclosing the television, the stripes of the chair cushions, and the accent pillows. An interesting touch is the wainscoting, which appears in the living room and continues throughout the cottage; in contrast to the tidy white walls, ceiling, and trim that have a shipshape look, the weathered wainscoting appears as if it were reclaimed wood with scraped white paint for a sense of age.

Upstairs, the same design scheme continues, with flat white paint on the board walls and ceilings, faded blue-green painted wooden plank floors, and the distressed reclaimed wood wainscoting. Pegs at the top of the stairs hold utilitarian canvas bags that are handy to load up for trips to the beach or to consolidate items that will be carried downstairs.

The master's soft yellow departs from the nautical theme. Reinforcing the sense of history and place, a toy Ferris wheel is a reminder of the amusement park that was once on a nearby boardwalk.

Cottages remind us of an important lesson: recognize when there is enough.
These two small, cheerful bedrooms provide all that's necessary.

Bright, saturated colors of mangoes, papayas, and citrus playfully echo the South Florida tropical setting to make this family home a joy for entertaining and spending time together.

Typical to some areas on the South Florida coast, this cottage home backs to a saltwater canal that feeds to the Intracoastal Waterway, which in turn connects to lagoons and the Atlantic. The family has boats moored at their own dock to explore these watery connections. From the front of the home, one would never know it is on the water, nor would anyone guess the vivid combinations of color and interesting rooms inside and the varied entertainment areas in the back.

A classic sedate bungalow on the outside, beautiful tropical colors liven it on the inside for a distinctive design.

In contrast to cottages that have a unified color and design theme throughout, distinctive colors set the mood in each room. One of the most unusual colorations is in the dining room, with warm red-pink walls. Distinctive wall colors give definition to each of the rooms, while the common wood flooring and white painted woodwork connect and unify the design.

ABOVE: The color selection makes the dining room a captivating space for a dinner party. Rather than matching the dining set, the sideboard is painted white.

OPPOSITE: From the entry, high ceilings and rich, vibrant tropical colors dominate the great room. To the rear, the red-pink dining room is set to the right and the kitchen is to the left.

One side of the main floor is dedicated to the children. A fun playroom has plenty of floor space for inventive play and furniture for curling up and relaxing. In one corner is a table for puzzles and projects, and the banquette seating has storage beneath the bench to keep the toys tidy but conveniently close. The children's bedrooms open to the playroom.

OPPOSITE: The bungalow's deep, broad porch is a wonderful place to sit in the shade and to keep an eye on children playing in the front yard.

ABOVE: Bins under the bench of the banquette provide easy storage for playthings.

RIGHT: Comfy seating across the way from the small table allows for multiple simultaneous activities.

ABOVE: French doors open from the master bedroom onto the patio.

The girls' bedroom rethinks closet storage for small children. With closet doors removed, there is room in one closet for a handsome armoire and in the other a nook for a striped chest of drawers. Over time, when a closet is needed, the doors can easily be returned.

The focus of this home is outdoor living, as evidenced by all the doors leading to the patio. The outdoor living space is furnished to maximize enjoyment, with a bar, conversation groupings, and tables for outdoor living. Truly it's a home for lively gatherings, with its happy punch of tropical color.

White window frames and mullions punctuate the green exterior, drawing attention to the architecture of this home. The outdoor area is set for partying!

Stylish furnishings on this pergola-covered deck make for an elegant outdoor room..

POLYCHROME PANACHE

Vivid varicolored walls and ceilings, as well as arched windows, courtyards, and accents, reminiscent of Florida's Spanish Colonial past, make this home a coastal Florida gem in a setting of tropical foliage and flowers.

Stepping into this South Florida home, one is welcomed with colors and patterns, giving the same treat to the senses as would walking into a garden filled with blossoms and blooms. Near the grand piano, two geometrically patterned sofas set at 90 degrees and a pair of deep papaya-colored skirted slipper chairs surround the glass-topped wrought iron coffee table. Interspersed tropical plants and flowers, brilliantly colored art pieces, and bright tangerine-striped drapes pepper the scene with even more color.

The front door opens to a vibrant living area, and further back is a formal dining area. Two doors on the far wall lead to the kitchen and the family room.

OPPOSITE: The dining area's colored and etched pendant bowl light, the artwork, and the details on the sideboard all add to the ornateness of the setting.

ABOVE: French doors in the main living area open to the covered porch sitting room off the master bedroom.

The family room gets extra comfortable and casual with wicker furniture and ample cushions. The coffee table has louvered plantation shutter panels on the sides to echo the design theme. But the big impact is color. Intense blue and yellow, from opposite sides of the color wheel, provide maximum contrast and tension. The open rafters are painted white, as are the cabinets and window and door moldings. The use of white for these elements repeats in the kitchen and bedrooms to offer continuity despite the other variations in color.

The family room is less formal and designed for relaxation. The banquette at the opposite side of the room offers an informal place for dining.

RIGHT: The kitchen has wide walkways between the counters and the stainless steel-topped island. This ample space allows for a number of people to work together in the kitchen for a communally prepared meal without getting in each other's way.

OPPOSITE: This covered porch is protected from wind and other elements on three sides but is open on one side to the patio. It serves as a private sitting room. Through the door and behind shear lace curtains is a glimpse of the papaya walls of the master bedroom.

A wide entrance from the family room connects the large kitchen. For continuity, the deep blue-violet wall color from the family room repeats on the kitchen wall, looking crisp against the white woodwork. The cabinet fronts are louvered (like plantation shutters), repeating an element used in the family room's coffee table and the exterior shutters. The cabinets are distress painted to give them a sense of age and time. The metal range backsplash is geometrically patterned and, again, slightly ornate. In a variation from the family room, the kitchen ceiling is sky blue, with a skylight in the center to provide natural light on the work area. The clerestory above the cabinets allows for even more natural light.

*White moldings,
drapes, and ceiling
rafters outline the
pleasing shapes
in the room.*

The generous master bedroom connects to the patio and pool outside to a sitting room porch, covered and enclosed on three sides but open to the yard on the third, and to the living and dining room. The room is spacious; in addition to the bed and ornate armoire, there is a chaise reading area and a tall bookcase desk. The colors can loosely be described as orange, with the walls of the room closer to papaya, the ceiling apricot, and the spread tangerine.

The heart of this home is the backyard with pool. Lined with palm trees and surrounded by flowering plants, it's a little bit of its own resort paradise in the backyard. Water spills over the stacked-stone edge of the hot tub and creates that wonderful falling water sound that masks ambient noise like traffic or a neighbor's power gardening tools.

A balcony with a white railing looks over the pool. The balcony leads inside to a bright aqua-blue bedroom with a contrasting red spread in the children's room. It appears that the children have the best view in the house, as the room looks over the treetops to the sea.

OPPOSITE: The lively tension between the bright aqua blue and red make this an unforgettable space.

ABOVE: The pool, hot tub, patio, and surrounding greenery take up most of the backyard.
With a resort-like setting such as this one, what more could one ask for?

When is a deck a dock? The answer to this riddle is when a home's outdoor living stretches over the water on pylons, and the deck ends at the water's edge.

With its prim New England shape and extended porch, this cottage looks like it might belong north of its Manasquan, New Jersey, setting. However, Manasquan has an interesting status in Atlantic shoreline communities, as it is at the northern terminus of the Intracoastal Waterway, which extends all the way north from Florida. It also has a summer cottage tradition dating back to the turn of the twentieth century, when some New York City families would summer in Manasquan, with the breadwinners working in the city during the week and taking the commuter train to visit their vacationing families each weekend.

Even a cloudy day at this colorful home couldn't be anything but cheerful. White paint outlines the lovely architectural shapes.

From the edge of the home to the edge of the water, the outdoor living space is maximized with tables for outdoor dining, conversation groupings, and lounges for basking in the sun, with a boat and barbecue mixed in for good measure. A deep covered porch with fans and lighting makes an all-weather outdoor space that can be used late into the evening.

ABOVE: The white wicker settee, chairs, and ottoman encircle the table with its small fire pit indented in the center for evening enjoyment.

RIGHT: Flowers mark the steps for the side entry to the home, where bikes are at the ready for running errands and exploring.

The designated entry is on the side of the home, which is handy from the parking in the alley. The entire lower level is one large open space encompassing the great room and kitchen. Three French doors connect the great room to the spacious waterside outdoor living area. Inside, a soft sofa and two chairs by the fireplace maintain views to the outdoors. There is a dining set to the side of the fireplace, but it is clear that for larger gatherings and entertaining, the preferred dining is outside.

ABOVE: With the whites and sand tones of the sofa, walls, and trim, the views outside become the natural visual focal points of the room.

OPPOSITE: A long rectangular bar with seafoam-green bar stools separates the kitchen from the rest of the great room.

DESIGN TIP: In homes with an open floor plan, creating a private corner, room for an out-of-the-way sofa, or a window seat allow space for privacy and recharging for those who need it.

The stairs, located between the main entry and the French doors, lead to the second level. There, the spacious master bedroom stretches the full width of the home, and a balcony, located atop the covered patio, overlooks the water.

OPPOSITE: The airy master bedroom is set directly above the great room. Large sliding doors open to the balcony, which sits on top of the roof over the patio, extending its width.

ABOVE LEFT: The sunny guest room is spacious enough for a pleasant seating area.

ABOVE RIGHT: Inside the alcove beneath the main floor's stairway is a vertically striped chest that works harmoniously with the vertical boards of the wainscoting. Storage in a small home is scarce and should be claimed whenever possible.

For the person who just loves everything about living on the shore—beach parties, dancing on the sand to the rifts of a surf band, swimming, combing the beach for shells and sea glass, afternoons on the boardwalk, and of course surfing—this might be the perfect home.

There are many mystiques about living on the ocean, and one is living the big surf party lifestyle portrayed in early '60s films of friends, music, surfing, and beach bonfires. Some things just don't go out of style. With the call "surf's up," this mid-Atlantic coastal home empties out, and like the tide, friends pour back in when the hosts beckon "party's on."

A tin-roofed beach bar is party ready, complete with a sandy beach for dancing. What look like beach changing rooms are cleverly disguised garden sheds.

LEFT: The wide porch gives a friendly look to the cottage. Surprisingly, there is a second level for bedrooms and an attic game room on top.

ABOVE: The living room has ample books and comfortable furnishings for a rainy day. The surfboard and snapshots of beach fun would make the family even more eager for the rains to end and to return to the shore.

The home opens to the living room, furnished with casual cushioned wicker and rattan furniture painted in shades of blue and blue green. The wooden plank floor, white ceilings, white window and door frames, and pale yellow walls appear throughout the three levels of the home; the white wainscoting is a common element on the ground floor.

From the living room, the home continues in a long, open rectangle to include a dining area and a kitchen. A circular braided rug defines the dining area, and the painted round table sits on top with a ship-inspired pendant light above. The spacious open kitchen has a peninsula with stools that makes a slight separation of the kitchen from the dining room.

The open shelves display family photos and personal collectibles, which give the home a story and make it more interesting. Storage space in small homes is always at a premium, and without enough storage (or with too much stuff), a cottage can feel cluttered. The cabinets provide a handy place to tuck away things like table linens, large serving dishes, holiday accessories, board games, and photo albums.

OPPOSITE: The kitchen has a farmhouse-style plan, with supporting farmhouse detailing like an apron-front sink, latch cabinet hardware, and painted cabinets with slat faces.

ABOVE: An assortment of bottles and vases filled with found pieces of sand-polished and etched glass that wash up on the beach decorates the space above the cabinets.

LEFT: Returning to the beach party theme of the backyard, Gidget and the gang appear in the kitchen poster.

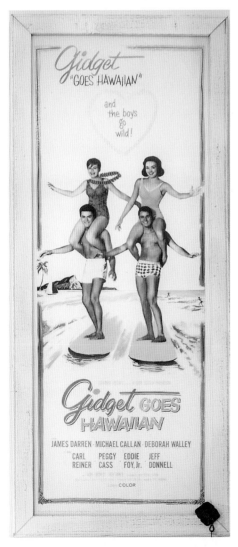

Upstairs on the second floor are bedrooms, and the third floor attic is a game room with a working vintage pinball machine and casual seating for watching television and playing video games. Fun is never too far away in this home!

The bedrooms feature painted furniture and wicker, white painted woodwork, and pale yellow walls consistent with the color palette downstairs.

DESIGN TIP: Decor need not be expensive to bring personality and life to your vacation home. For example, at far right, a simple strand of beach fence has been attached to the wall, and vacation snapshots of all the people and fun times can be rotated on and off throughout the season.

ABOVE: Tucked in a corner by the staircase is a working pinball machine, and mounted on the wall above the stairs is the brilliant salvaged face of another pinball game.

RIGHT: The living room has a display of whole bottles.

BREEZY AND DEMURE

Straightforward and consistent materials, a basic shotgun floor plan, and restrained but confident furnishings, mingle simplicity with sophistication.

One of the great cottage traditions is that a vacation home takes a backseat to the beautiful location where it is located—meaning the focus of the occupants is on the place they are exploring, not on possessions or the lavishness of their home. This cottage in a mid-Atlantic coastal village beautifully embodies the spirit of maintaining cottage simplicity.

The living room introduces common elements that appear throughout the home: the white-painted board-and-batten walls, the plank ceiling with exposed rafters, and the wooden plank floor, which is painted forest green with a gloss finish on the ground floor and shifts to red on the second floor. As with many cottages, white and the continuation of color unites it and makes the home feel more spacious.

The living room exudes ease and relaxation with its cushioned furniture, soft colors, and the hint of a floral motif, which appears in the upholstery of the yellow-apricot paired chairs and the painting. The cabinets and shelves on the wall by the stove make it additionally homey, with a scattering of books and mementos.

LEFT: The base level of this home is clapboard and the upper level is shingled. Tin covers the porch at the front and the roof of the bay window for a practical, modest look. Clean lines carefully maintain the scale to give it a crisp quality.

OPPOSITE: Comfort and relaxation start with a deep, inviting porch.

Entering the home on the left side, the rooms are layered in the style of shotgun homes of New Orleans, but with a variation: unlike shotgun homes, the rooms articulate on the side of the home instead of the center, and there are ample windows along this side. The opposite side, which is close to a neighboring house, has minimal windows and only at the back.

At one time the family room, above, was the last room on the main level. When a family member who could not use the stairs moved in, a new addition provided another bedroom. Instead of blending the added bedroom with the rest of the house, the approach used was to make it an obvious addition with an entirely different design approach—tropical.

ABOVE: Beyond the kitchen, a cozy family room allows for some TV time while others in the house may visit without the interruption.

OPPOSITE: Knotty pine and tropical colors set this room apart as an addition and a comfortable guest space.

ABOVE: An efficient kitchen is measured by the fewest steps within the kitchen triangle. Here, the distances between the farmhouse sink, range, and refrigerator are minimal.

OPPOSITE: An airy dining space sits just behind the living area and opposite the kitchen.

Upstairs, the painted wood floors are a deep, glossy red. A short hallway with a home office links the two upstairs bedrooms.

ABOVE & OVERLEAF: The bedrooms each retain a consistency with the overall design of white-planked ceilings and softer white paint on the vertical wood of the walls. The seaside accessories complement the rooms without overwhelming them.

COTTAGE FOR TWO

This romantic cottage right on the beach has just enough space for two to have a splendid time.

There's a touch of a honeymoon quality about this compact rectangular cottage, and rightly so, as the architect took his inspiration from Thomas Jefferson's Honeymoon Cottage, the small home where Jefferson lived while designing and building Monticello. Built just behind the sandy dunes on the beach at Seaside, Florida, it connects with its ocean setting with wide views to the gulf from the top deck at the rear.

The stairs by the front door lead up to the linear kitchen and dining space, a living area, and the broad portico. The interior is less than 800 square feet in size, but the broad portico upstairs and the covered porch downstairs substantially increase the space for relaxing.

The portico cornice over the front entry pays tribute to Thomas Jefferson's Honeymoon Cottage in Virginia, its inspiration. Sand leads right up to the doorway, while the native landscaping, a hallmark of Seaside, Florida, grows to the side.

This cottage is a study in efficient use of space, as one living area flows into another without walls or partitions. For example, the chairs may be pulled back once meal preparation is complete, for a spacious table that seats four. The vertical piece of fabric art above the wicker tea table (which delightfully stores the table linens) declares the shift from the kitchen to the living area.

OPPOSITE & ABOVE LEFT: The kitchen is a study in efficiency. With the stairway behind the counter and cooktop area, there is no room for upper cabinets. A wooden armoire supplements storage with a place for the microwave and additional shelves for food.

ABOVE RIGHT: The tea cart and vertical fabric mark the transition from the kitchen to the living area. The tea table and adjacent wicker hamper provide additional storage.

A fringed oval rug in a pale sandy hue anchors the living area as a conversation grouping. The sofa and chairs have matching slipcovers—a great beach furnishing treatment because they are easily washed. Also, many vacation cottage furnishings have a history and don't match until they don slipcovers

The memorable portico is a step outside from the living room. Covered, but open on three sides, the space opens to the sea air and hovers over the surrounding beach. To adapt to conditions, there are drapes that close on the sides. The furnishings inspire relaxing here all day with the sectional sofa and ottoman and a wrought iron bistro set.

OPPOSITE: Slipcovers throughout the house tie the furniture into a clean group that is at once elegant and casual, even though chairs and sofas may have different histories and styles.

ABOVE: The outdoor living space combines the best of indoor comforts while enjoying closeness to the sky, sea, and sand.

The bedroom suite is on the lower level along with its en suite bath and connecting lower porch. All in white with soft fabrics, the bedroom invokes its inspiration as a honeymoon cottage.

In contrast to the upstairs outdoor living area, the downstairs screened porch is a much more private place with a jetted soaking tub. Slatted folding shutters close for more privacy or to adapt to the weather. Another pleasant touch, a nostalgic hanging swing offers a perfect place to sip a cup of tea and read. All the spaces work harmoniously for an enchanting vacation retreat.

LEFT: In an all-white room, variations are achieved through shapes and textures like the curving wrought iron headboard and footboard and the similar curves of the bedside table. The white painted ceiling has extra depth because of the exposed rafters.

ABOVE: Screened by the sand dune's native vegetation, the lower porch is a private hideaway.

QUINTESSENTIALLY CARMEL

Homegrown through a series of additions, this garden cottage represents many distinctive features of the cottages in Carmel-by-the-Sea.

Located midway on the California coast on the Monterey Peninsula, Carmel-by-the-Sea has for more than a hundred years attracted an exciting group of creative spirits along with academics from Stanford and Berkeley who have summered here. Inexpensive housing was developed by innovating cottages ranging from fairy-tale inspirations to the simple honesty of Arts and Crafts bungalows and many styles in between.

Displaying a Spanish influence, the U shape of this home wraps around a central courtyard. Six doors connect the rooms of the home to the courtyard, which is an extended living area that can be enjoyed most of the year. The home's siding varies from stucco to board-and-batten, and this tells a story of progressive additions over the years.

The split Dutch door at the front entry is common in Carmel. In this mild Mediterranean climate, the top can be left open and the closed bottom portion can keep two- and four-legged critters on the preferred side of the door.

The entry leads to the living room, which exudes casual elegance and comfort. Many of the design elements in this room continue throughout the home, such as the restored original walnut hardwood floors, the rustic ceiling timbers, white woodwork, arches, and wide double glass-paned doors.

OPPOSITE: The console table fills the wide archway to the bedroom hallway. The treatment and lighting create the appearance of an alcove.

LEFT: The fireplace is constructed from Carmel stone, a limestone quarried locally. The mantel beam was found on the property. To the right, the double doors lead to the dining room, and the doors to the left go to the rear courtyard.

ABOVE: Many of the homes in Carmel have low roofs. To compensate, the rooms are open to the roof pitch and often the roof supports are visible.

The homeowner incorporated a number of antiques throughout the home, offsetting the hard edges and weathered look of the antiques with new, softly upholstered furniture. The look is one of comfort, where nothing looks either too new or old and tired.

The dining room sits between the living room and kitchen, and it also has doors to the back courtyard for outside dining. Because of this arrangement, the room gets a lot of foot traffic. The small circular table was selected to allow for circulation through the room.

Beginning with a single room probably dating from the late 1800s, a succession of additions through the last century expanded this cottage. The most recent update sought to restore design integrity throughout the home for a sense of wholeness.

LEFT & ABOVE: The bedrooms illustrate the homeowner's style of softening and brightening rooms with ample new soft bedding as an offset to the antique furniture pieces. Weathered shutters on the interior is an interesting approach to the window treatments. They are used on the exterior to make the presence of the windows seem larger, and they accomplish the same purpose inside.

ABOVE: The sounds of tumbling water from the fountain can be heard throughout the home.

OPPOSITE: Not wanting to include functional doors to the courtyard, a low planter blocks entry, but the room still benefits from doors open to fresh air and the early morning bird songs.

ROSES AND LAVENDER

92

Located on a point reaching out into Puget Sound, this coastal garden cottage is surrounded by roses and lavender that date to before the home.

Whidbey Island, Washington, has a beautiful winding coast of beaches and inlets, and it offers a wonderful backdrop of evergreens and rolling land. Nestled in a carefully nurtured and thriving garden of roses and lavender that was on the land before the home was built, this board-and-batten white cottage looks out to the sound and Camano Island. Behind, the evergreens of the hillside are homes to bald eagles, great blue herons, and colorful songbirds that call as they fly over the cottage.

The home is oriented linearly, and with the varying roof pitches, it appears from a distance as an assemblage of tiny cottages. At the near end are the sitting area and kitchen, with a shed roof covering the porch nearest the water. The central portion has a welcoming front entry, and to the left of the door are a bedroom and a bath. Moving right, the lowered roof pitch makes it appear like a breezeway to the garage, but this section comprises the master bedroom. Above the garage, in what appears to be a caretaker's room, is a painter's studio and storage.

UPPER LEFT: Walking down the pathway from the front door one can soak in a view of where the beach curves inland from the point.

LEFT: A nook by the front entry provides convenient storage for hats, jackets, and beach gear.

In the sitting room, the row of paned glass windows captures the views in a panorama. With the furnishings clustered in a conversation grouping near the stove the room feels cozy, but at the same time the height of the room adds a sense of being open and unconfined. The Whidbey Island architect who designed the cottage is known for capturing the utmost in natural light, and here he vaulted the ceiling to the rafters. A horizontal board continues the line of the upper window frames and lowers the scale of the room to compensate for the high ceiling.

The accessories and row of shell sconces follow a seaside theme.

The kitchen is opposite the sitting room, and the kitchen island serves to separate the spaces. The décor continues the same color scheme of white with splashes of blue, and the same tone of wood used on the floor repeats on the tops of the island and counters. Pendants light the work surfaces and hang to the height of the horizontal elements in the room. The shell sconces continue from the sitting room to the kitchen to connect the spaces as a whole.

ABOVE: Built-in benches flank the long pedestal table with windows enclosing it on three sides. A chandelier dresses it up a bit.

OPPOSITE. The large island and counter provide ample workspace.

DESIGN TIP: Adding nooks and shelves makes a meaningful difference by making the home more interesting. They add charm and allow personal touches like showing off home-canned pickles.

The kitchen has 1930s-era charm because of the detailing in the woodwork and the open shelves. The appliances by Heartland, while new, are vintage in their appearance and scaled just right.

OPPOSITE: Combining the best of both the past and present, the kitchen has the charm of a bygone era but an efficient design and brand-new appliances.

Between the front entry and the sitting room and kitchen are a bedroom and the main bathroom for the home. Past the entry is the master bedroom suite with an office area and a half bathroom.

OPPOSITE: In the master bedroom suite, a built-in desk makes use of corridor space for a home office. A framed doorway and low wall give seeming separation to the bedroom without blocking air circulation or natural light.

ABOVE: The painted iron headboard and quilted spread add a timeless feel.

ABOVE: A stone path leads around to the back of the house and expands into a patio in the garden.

OPPOSITE: A wicker seating area on a covered porch off the kitchen overlooks the roses and out to Puget Sound.

PLACE REMEMBERED

Ties to a turn-of-the-century fisherman's lodge can be seen in this Whidbey Island cottage with its broad porches, hipped roof, and traditional island-green color.

The site for the cottage was a natural choice. The homeowner's family has a vacation cottage in the same small private enclave on Whidbey Island's curving beach by Greenbank. He grew up exploring and loving the area.

At the turn of the twentieth century, there had been a fisherman's lodge, the Greenbank Hotel, on this property, where guests came to stay and tried their luck at crabbing and fishing. Photographs and stories presented clear images of what it looked like: a deep wraparound porch, hipped roof, and the traditional island building style popular between 1890 and 1930. The small hotel was painted green, one of just a few color choices to be found on the island at that time. The fisherman's lodge became the inspiration for this cottage, which the homeowner calls the Greenbank Lodge.

The wooden clapboard home has a generous overhang to shade the upper windows midday, a deep covered porch furnished with two large picnic tables, and views to the beach and the water. Two doors open to unite the interior with the porch for an easy flow.

The home delivers on the homeowners' wish for simplicity to be the heart of how they live—to be at ease, with no pretensions. The design also recognizes the family's desire as to how they like to

ABOVE: A compass rose is inlaid in the wooden floor between the adjoining dining and living areas.

RIGHT: Not to be overlooked, the family pet has positioned himself strategically by the entrance to the kitchen and with the hallway behind him that leads to the side door, two bedrooms, and a den.

OPPOSITE: Sunrise is through the sitting room windows, and with the morning's cool temperatures, the upholstery and cushions bring welcome warmth.

For the transition to evening, the sconces and chandelier add to the ambience,
as does the glow of the lighting in the glass-fronted upper cabinet where
some of the most interesting glassware and serving pieces are displayed.

spend their time. The front entry opens to a space that spreads the width of the cottage. At one side is the sitting area, with seating gathered around the fireplace and mementoes of the family's experiences and travels, and on the other side is a big dining table for hosting the family and friends with whom they love to share the experience of staying at the beach on the island.

The high ceiling, transom windows, and clerestory fill the room with natural light and views to the beach, Puget Sound, and Camano Island, and at the same time make it feel spacious. Whidbey Island is far enough north that the change of season brings short days, and sitting in front of the fire is perfect during the long evenings.

The dining room demonstrates carefully planned circulation. The double front doors and a side door open to the wraparound porch, and the opening to the kitchen serves multiple functions: a bar for seating, a pass-through to the dining room for setting the table and serving, and a place to lay out a buffet. It also shields any meal preparation clutter in the kitchen.

The long galley kitchen has work surfaces on both sides and plenty of storage to make it highly functional.

LEFT: The rear of the home is quiet, and a writing desk by the window offers a place to journal or catch up with correspondence.

ABOVE: The family room to the rear of the cottage, with its low wooden ceiling, has a different feel from the front sitting room. It's a place for private relaxation like reading or needlework.

With sailors, fishermen, gardeners, and beachcombers coming and going, the working entrance to the home is on the side and connects with the mudroom. Surrounding the bench is additional storage in the form of hooks and a shelf carved and shaped like that of a boat. The home's architect, Ross Chapin, FAIA, has written that in a small home, the space has to perform. "As in a boat, everything has to be well fitted with a place and purpose."

OPPOSITE: Benches make it possible to change footwear before going inside.

ABOVE: Looking out the doorway, a low stone wall protects the grass and plants from Puget Sound's waves at high tide. The residual pylons from an old private dock in the distance and the carefully conserved grand old elm tree serve as reminders of the place's history.

Passersby walking the meandering, rocky shoreline road are drawn to this picturesque stone cottage built in 1928, when artists, painters, musicians, writers, poets, and thespians were the majority of Carmel-by-the-Sea's lively population.

The stone and redwood home has changed little from when it was built in 1928, and it offers a glimpse into Carmel's past. It is a home that has inspired loyal affection from the two families who have owned and cared for it, and the native straight-grained redwood and Carmel stone are in place as they were ninety years ago.

The protruding half-hexagon southern wall of the home shapes this end of the living room. It allows windows to face three directions for 180-degree views. To the left the views look to the side courtyard (the one with the arched, gated entry); forward, it takes in the coastline to the south; and to the right it directly faces the sea.

ABOVE: The near end (right) of the one-story portion of the home is shaped as half a hexagon, essentially making the entire end of the home function as a bay window.

OPPOSITE: Set on the shoreline, only a scenic lane separates the stone cottage from the cliff and rocky beach, which can be glimpsed through the arched entry from the stone courtyard in the side garden.

The original family kept the home for 40 years. A couple who saw the cottage while on their Carmel honeymoon, and had ever since dreamed of owning it, finally bought it over 25 years later in 1968. While many Carmel cottages were and continue as vacation cottages, this one is a primary residence.

It's common to see walkers stop to admire the home and take pictures, and occasionally artists can be seen with their easels, sketching and painting. Popular artist Thomas Kinkade was one, and he romantically embellished his painting of the cottage with a lush hollyhock garden and vines.

Tempered by the Pacific Ocean, Carmel has a pleasantly mild climate year-round. It allows for the home's opening casement windows without screens, French doors to the courtyard, and split Dutch door. The original stone and redwood remain, with the redwood still fresh inside and weathered to a gray on some of the exterior. The elongated black hinges on the front door are original hardware, as are the latch on the side door and interior hardware throughout the home.

ABOVE: A stone path winds around the home's kitchen and tower.

OPPOSITE: The side door adjacent to the tower has a split Dutch door, which is common in Carmel homes. The exterior redwood has weathered to gray where it is exposed to the sun and salty air, while the protected beams and door frame retain the wood's rich color. Redwood is known for its resistance to decay and fire.

The front door opens to the spacious living room, where the vaulted redwood ceiling opens to the rafters. The copper fireplace hood immediately catches the eye. The first owner brought the copper hood and the copper lantern fixtures from Germany to be included in the home, and he had the chimney built specifically for the hood. The chimney is structural to the house, supporting the roof.

Initially, the fireplaces were the only heat in the home and were necessary to take off the morning chill and to keep it comfortable during the evenings. When the home was first constructed, an ingenious system of coils in the chimney heated the water.

OPPOSITE: The first owner custom-built the chimney to fit the copper fireplace hood, which he imported from Germany.

ABOVE: The western-facing living room windows provide an unobstructed view to the sea.

The kitchen is located just behind the tower; it has a shed roof and ample windows. The second owners updated the kitchen at least 45 years ago, and it has been unchanged since that update, including the appliances.

Adjacent to the living room is the dining room in the tower, with its ceilings lower than the living room. The hutch is redwood, as are the ceiling planks and beams. Two side-hinged casement windows swing open to welcome the breezes. The views from these windows include the coast north to Monterey and Pebble Beach.

ABOVE: The small desk in the kitchen intended for researching recipes benefits from the fresh air from the operable window in the corner, which offers views in two directions.

OPPOSITE: The dining room has an early California look resulting from the arched alcoves with shelves and the planked, open-beamed ceiling.

A breezeway lined with Carmel stone runs behind the living room and connects to the side courtyard with French doors. Off the breezeway is a den with nearly floor-to-ceiling windows and its own doorway to the courtyard. The wooden accordion doors can close off the breezeway.

OPPOSITE: At the opposite end of the den, sliding doors can close off the office. The photographs are by Ansel Adams, a twentieth-century photographer who lived in the area.

ABOVE: The courtyard, breezeway, and den all connect in an informal part of the home that reflects the indoor-outdoor living connections that are so desirable in cottage homes.

Two staircases—one from the living room and the other from the breezeway—lead upstairs to three bedrooms. The master bedroom extends the width of the back of the cottage, and its ample size allows for a fireplace with a cluster of chairs and a writing desk. Paned casement windows encircle the room for treetop views and ventilation, and the vaulted redwood ceiling is similar to that of the living room.

*At the rear of the home and upstairs, the
master bedroom feels like a private cabin.*

This Santa Monica home challenges preconceptions of what a cottage is and isn't.

It didn't take long for Santa Monica to become a resort destination. Lured by the perfect temperatures and the coastline around Santa Monica Bay, by the early 1900s it was a hopping place with a pier and ballroom to add to the fun for vacationers and beachgoers. Los Angeles being only a short 16-mile trip inland, Santa Monica soon grew to be more than a resort, with prosperity from the aircraft industry, film studios, the music business, and now, tech businesses.

Perfect land for a beach home in a populated area wasn't to be had, and that made this slimly confined lot next to an old beach cottage quite a find while raising the question of how to build on it.

The resulting linear contemporary design made the most of the 25-foot width. The main floor soars two levels, with a railed gallery mid-level. The high ceilings keep the space light and airy despite the

This tightly narrow lot right on the beach nestles closely next to an early beach cottage. In acknowledgment of its neighbor, the new top roof pitch matches the one next door. In front is the beach walk, which is heavily trafficked with runners, skaters, cyclists, baby joggers, and a parade of colorful activities. To achieve privacy, the first floor and deck are elevated, with a low wall shielding part of the outdoor deck facing the beach.

narrow width. The wall facing the beach is a glass roll-up door. With a building situated tightly on one side, the architect avoided clear windows in favor of frosted translucent panes that admit natural light. The opposite side provides a sizable section of windowless wall for the homeowners' painting. Outdoor seating flows into the living area to allow for entertaining more than just a few.

The open floor plan layers the living area, with the most public functions closest to the outdoors. Nearest the patio is a fireplace to anchor the living space. The sofa and chairs are clustered on an area rug. While the color of the rug is close to that of the wood floors to merge the space and make it feel larger, the rug still subtly defines the seating area. The chairs are

OPPOSITE: You can appreciate the views and the changing light of the sky from anywhere in the open area, but the living area is closest to the grand opening in the wall for the greatest enjoyment. The fireplace warms the space, so the overhead garage door may be kept open even on cooler evenings.

ABOVE: The floating white stairway with its absent risers adds to the transparency by minimizing obstruction to the light entering through the wall of frosted panes.

lightweight and easily moved to give flexibility for entertaining.

The dining area achieves a greater intimacy because the railed gallery lowers the ceiling. Shelves and a galley kitchen are to the rear of the space, tucked away behind a partial wall that is well sized for the artwork.

Because of the absence of walls to segment the small space, there is room for a grand piano without feeling crowded. The stairway leads up to the gallery and to the bedrooms on the third floor.

DESIGN TIP: Artwork is key to a room's design, not an accessory added after the design is complete. These large, dramatic art pieces charge the energy of the home and are key to all the other selections. Different art would make for an entirely different experience in the home.

The ceiling for the mezzanine gallery lowers the scale and allows for an interesting effect. The gallery is broad enough for furnishings, including a desk. Below the back gallery is the entrance to the kitchen. A house for two or a crowd, the partial wall shields the kitchen activity and maintains an undisturbed entertainment space.

ABOVE: *Perched above the main living area, the master bedroom enjoys privacy and connects to its own patio. The white-on-white color scheme is serene and makes the view outside the focal point of the room.*

OPPOSITE: *It's a small home with strong connections to the outdoors, but the forms are geometric and modern, and there isn't space for a garden.*

LOFTY HAVEN

At the seashore, the ground-hugging mist breaks up in dreamlike colors, inspiring the soft colors inside this tall, elegant but simple cottage.

Set in a mid-Atlantic seaside vacation community, the cottage is separated from an ocean bay only by a low spit. The generous windows on the upper two levels capture views of the surroundings. While the home benefits from the views, more direct influences for its stacked design were the confined size and shape of the lot and the need to build a house essentially on pylons to withstand storm surges from hurricanes and destructive tides.

While growing up, the homeowner, cousins, and friends spent summers in the same beach town at the family's vacation home. Sadly, Superstorm Sandy destroyed the old family home, and the homeowner searched to find a site in the same town to rebuild. This shallow, narrow lot is restricted on one side by a crushed-shell driveway and to the back by a small home. Despite the lot's small size, the advantages were the proximity to the water and the friendly neighbors in the two adjacent cottages. With such a small footprint, space could only be found by going up.

An entry stairway at the side of the home climbs the outer wall to the second level above the garage. The front door opens into a view of the unexpected whimsical space in a delightful surprise. Carefully planned, the living space is all above the garage level.

Because of setbacks and easements, the outdoor living space is limited to the footprint of the home behind the garage and within the home's pylon supports. Brightly painted beach furniture arranged in a circle makes for an inviting place to watch the last rays of the day together.

The main level consists of a living area, kitchen, laundry room, and to the rear of the home, the lovely shell-pink master bedroom. The living area faces the spit and the water, and sliding doors open for the sea breezes. The height of the room by the front extends through the floor above to the roof. Set back above the living room on the third floor is a den with sleeper sofas that allow it to double as a guest room. A window from the den looks out to the living room and through to the exterior windows. It allows for natural light, but the window blocks out sound between the two spaces.

ABOVE: The den's window looks out to the living room and gains light from the living room's row of clerestory windows while blocking out distractive noise common when a loft is left open.

RIGHT: One of two paintings in the living area that capture the mist of a foggy morning.

RIGHT: The high ceiling in the sitting area compensates for the narrowness of the building.

The floor of the cottage is whitewashed to brighten the space while still showing the knots and grain of the wood.

DESIGN TIP: Paint furniture to match or contrast paint tones for interest.

It's a cottage tradition to paint handed-down mismatched furniture to add similarity and make it a set. Here, painting two chairs orchid instead of sea foam green brings into the kitchen a color from the artwork and the furnishings in the living area. It celebrates the design's wonderful pastels and unites the open floor plan's colors.

The new home is timeless in style with white woodwork and simple forms. The design maximizes light through ample windows, and the white ceilings reflect it to make it seem brighter. The painted furniture and the pieces with a scalloped pattern lend playfulness to the space consistent with the use of the home as a weekend and vacation retreat.

ABOVE: In addition to the den upstairs, at the rear is a sunny guest room. To allow for more guests or to suit a couple with children, a partial wall and ceiling beam separate out a nook for two twin beds. It projects the feeling of history like an addition or an enclosed sleeping porch, but it is all new construction.

OPPOSITE: The shell-pink master bedroom is conducive to sleep and relaxation.

REFINED COMFORT

The influences of Swedish Classicism and traditional American wooden seaside vacation homes combine to give an uplifting elegance to a livable cottage home.

The combination of classical elements and a greater attention to architectural detailing with traditional early cottage building materials and colors combine to bring a refined accessibility to this three-level Seaside, Florida, cottage. The architect describes it as a balance of naiveté and sophistication. Two design influences mingle and can be seen throughout : 1930s Swedish Classicism and vernacular turn-of-the-century wooden American seaside resort houses.

Porches are a common (and required) design element of Seaside homes, and three large porches on the ocean side, one on each level, offer considerable outdoor living. While the interior spaces limit the size of the group one might be able to entertain, the outdoor living expands it. The style

Classic pillars give even an informal space an ageless dignity. The dune with natural vegetation seen beyond the railing separates the home from the beach and protects the home from the severe storms and surges that occasionally pound the beaches.

of outdoor living corresponds to the lifestyle in the adjacent portions of the home, where the middle, or main, floor is public, and the porches off the bedrooms are more private.

The beach's sand dunes obstruct the ocean view on the garden floor. In order to have views, the main living area is located on the second floor, or middle level. The side garden entrance opens to a small foyer, and from there a stairway leads to the main living area, where big double doors open to the covered outdoor living space and the ocean views and breezes. The ceilings are high, the colors are light, and there are ample operable windows and French double doors to keep the space feeling open and unconfined.

The ocean end of the long rectangle opens to a deep covered outdoor living area that extends the width of the home. The colors are similar to the interior, but the decking and outdoor furniture make it somewhat more casual on one hand, while the carved and fluted columns maintain a classic tone.

In contrast to the inscribed columns and the elegance of the woodwork and the classic furnishings in the living and dining room, the warm yellow kitchen has a touch of whimsy. Beyond its visual appeal, it is an efficient working kitchen. Counter space is generous, the apron-fronted farmhouse sink is deep, the range has ample burners, the oven is large enough for a holiday meal, and a pantry provides additional storage.

Upstairs on the top level is the master suite, which includes a generous private sitting area with a nook for a built-in sofa. It's an appealing solution to offer some extra privacy for the homeowners, since vacation cottages often host gatherings, holidays, and parties. This is an area to retreat to for a bit of quiet time when the home is filled with guests.

Two large doors lead out from the master to the open porch, which is furnished with a tall bistro table and stools, a conversational seating area, and lounges. A single column supports the trussed roof, which reaches partially over the space, leaving some sunny area for basking on the chaises.

The children's bedrooms are on the garden level of the home. One bedroom is set by itself at the end of the home, and the two on the opposite end connect with the screened porch. There are stronger hints of the Swedish Classicism influences in the two children's bedrooms that connect to the screened porch. The built-in bed enclosure with the trundle bed beneath is especially Swedish.

All the outdoor living faces the beach, but the dunes block the views from the lowest level. On the garden level is a screened porch off the children's bedrooms. The middle level has a large covered outdoor space off the living room that is essentially another living and dining room with views above the dunes to the beach and the ocean. A distinctive single central pillar marks the partially covered porch space off the master bedroom, a private space for sunning and relaxation.

ABOVE: Ascending the stairs from the garden level, an ocean view welcomes arrival to the middle level.

RIGHT: A softly patterned area rug unites the living and dining areas, and the sand tones of the rug and low sofa, chairs, and coffee table bring a quiet sense to the space. The white of the woodwork and drapes becomes a backdrop that focuses attention to the center of the room. These treatments plus the additional depth provided by viewing through to the kitchen make the space feel larger, a key design approach for cottages

OPPOSITE: The transition to the kitchen marks a shift in mood from the living and dining space. The ceiling is lower, the detailing is at a finer scale, and touches like the finials in the glass cabinet door moldings add charm.

UPPER & LOWER RIGHT: The kitchen spans the width of the cottage. On one end, double doors open to a narrow balcony and the screened doors allow fresh air. In the opposite direction, the refrigerator's pleasing cabinetry and furniture-styled feet blend it with the other cabinetwork. To the left is the pantry door.

LEFT: The master suite extends the width of the cottage, with the sleeping and sitting areas separated by a central access way to the private covered porch.

ABOVE: The engaging nook invites curling up with something to read and savoring some quiet moments. Even here, the design claims opportunities for storage by way of shelving and drawers beneath.

ABOVE AND OPPOSITE: The sleeping nook is a charming place for hanging out or sleeping. Functionally, the nook takes very little space and allows for furnishing a sitting area. French doors open to the screened porch.

ABOVE: The nook's lowered pitched ceiling over the bed makes this bedroom a cozy and memorable room. Built-in shelves provide extra storage and a place for odds and ends, keeping the space tidy.

The large diamond-shaped blue and white floor tiles mark the small entry foyer off the garden entrance. A door opens to a short hallway leading to a bedroom that is lined with storage on both sides. The architects alluded to a ship when designing the cottage, where it is important to make every square inch work.

The porch swing is perfect to while away idle hours, but in a pinch it is spacious enough for an overflow sleeping space for an extra guest.

The many options for sitting, conversation, and dining adjacent to the porch inspire a party, and the spacious kitchen makes it ideal for dining in.

Tall shuttered doors open from the sitting and dining spaces on the main floor to the sheltered front porch with its traditional rockers, and true to the plantation style, a second porch above connects with the home's bedrooms. The heart of the home is a kitchen that is as lovely as it is functional.

The cottage design is inspired by Southern plantations, and another way of looking at plantations is as farmhouses for Southern climes. This very practical design allows multiple double doors to open off both porches to maximize ventilation and open the pedestrian flow from the outside in. In the event of big storms, the porches offer a protective overhang and the shutters close. The main floor features an L-shaped open living space furnished to create distinct sitting spaces, with a dining area adjacent to the big farmhouse kitchen. But in addition to practicality, the plantation style resonates with the culture's emphasis on grace, hospitality, and classic beauty.

ABOVE: One conversation area pairs two sofas by bookcases in a television and game area.

OPPOSITE: A second sitting area is furnished with four chairs set by the fire,

The dining area offers a glimpse of the kitchen. There is an interesting play on colors in this transition. In the dining room the walls are blue-green with white trim, and in the kitchen the colors juxtapose to white walls and blue-green cabinets.

DESIGN TIP: Consider a glass dining tabletop for cottage furnishings to keep a light informality and to make the room appear larger and simpler because of its transparency. Tempered glass won't shatter, but it is important that the edges and corners are finished so they aren't sharp and are safe against impact, especially with children in the home.

Side-hinged casement windows open into the kitchen for ventilation and let in the sweet sea air. The kitchen offers a number of other convenience elements, such as the open plate racks, glass-fronted cabinets, and open shelving to store serving dishes. The floral skirting on the farmhouse sink and the matching fabric valence add to the charm. However, the stainless steel ultra quiet dishwasher is a reminder that as lovely as the kitchen appears, it is designed for efficiency.

ABOVE AND RIGHT: The upstairs bedroom's shell-pink color evokes the seashore, and the mirror above the dressing table has a frame of shells in the same pink.

OPPOSITE: Two sets of French doors open to porches from this bedroom: the one seen is on the rear of the home and the one on the opposite wall leads to the upstairs front porch and rockers.

The two bedrooms exude design ideas like placing photos under the glass vanity top, and letting seashore pastels play together in the colors of walls, ceilings, furnishings, and linens.

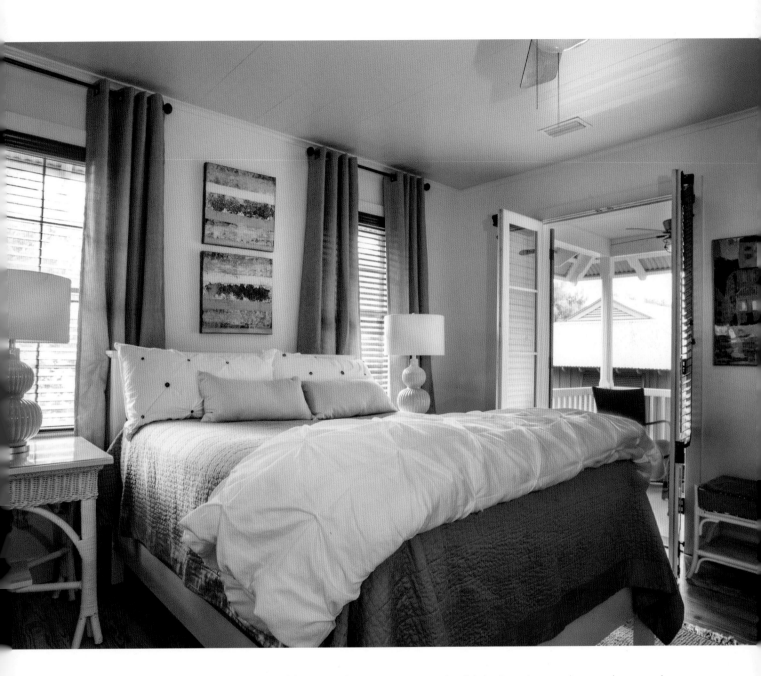

It is our hope that the homes featured here might inspire some playful designs in your home, dear reader, and that by looking through these pages you might feel a little sand between your toes and a yearn to walk through the breaking waves.

acknowledgments

We have found overwhelming kindness and generosity in the people who design, build, and live in cottages that made working on this book a true pleasure.

To our friend Marie Speed, thank you for your introductions. Robert Davis, who with Daryl Davis founded Seaside Florida, made our stay unforgettable. Lori Smith and Sarah Hanley managed all our arrangements.

Tom Bateman of Imagineered Homes answered a call from strangers and spent a week guiding, opening doors, and helping us. Marie Lupinski hosted our stay in her lovely brand-new cottage.

Ross Chapin, famous for his cottage designs, talked to us to help us better understand the detailing, materials, space planning, and care that make some cottages so memorable, and he introduced us to Joanne and Bruce Montgomery, who so generously accommodated us.

Art and architectural historian Kent Seavey helped us immensely in Carmel.

And to the homeowners of the many cottages we photographed, thank you for creating and sharing your beautiful homes and for allowing others to experience the delight of cottage living.

sources

Sailor's Life for Me

Design concepts, interior design, and construction:
Imagineered Homes
Manasquan, NJ
www.imagineeredhomes.com
(732) 207-5009 & (732) 528-9206

Architecture:
Imagineered Homes and Steve Duarte

Many furnishings:
Maine Cottage Furniture
www.mainecottage.com

Living on the Edge

Design concepts, interior design, and construction:
Imagineered Homes
Manasquan, NJ
www.imagineeredhomes.com
(732) 207-5009 & (732) 528-9206

Architecture:
Steve Duarte and Robert Dooley

Beachcomber's Party House

Design concepts, interior design, and construction:
Imagineered Homes
Manasquan, NJ
www.imagineeredhomes.com
(732) 207-5009 & (732) 528-9206

Architecture:
Imagineered Homes and Steve Duarte

Breezy and Demure

Design concepts, interior design, and construction:
Imagineered Homes
Manasquan, NJ
www.imagineeredhomes.com
(732) 207-5009 & (732) 528-9206

Architecture:
Imagineered Homes and Rick Thompson

Many furnishings:
Maine Cottage Furniture
www.mainecottage.com

Cottage for Two

Architecture:
Scott Merrill
Merrill, Pastor & Colgan
Vero Beach, FL
(772) 492-1983
www.merrillpastor.com

Rentals:
Coordinated by Cottage Rental Agency
Seaside, FL
www.cottagerentalagency.com

Quintessentially Carmel

Design and Renovation:
Mary Capson
Capson Associates
Carmel, CA

Roses and Lavender

Architecture:
Ross Chapin, FAIA,
Ross Chapin Architects
Langley, WA
www.rosschapin.com

Construction:
Richard S. Epstein
Whidbey Island, WA
www.richardsepstein.com

Place Remembered

Architecture:
Ross Chapin, FAIA,
Ross Chapin Architects
Langley, WA
www.rosschapin.com

Construction:
Richard S. Epstein
Whidbey Island, WA
www.richardsepstein.com

Nowhere But Up

Architecture:
Steven Ehrlich, FAIA, RIBA,
Ehrlich, Yanai, Rhee, Chaney Architects
Culver City, CA
www.eyrc.com

Lofty Haven

Design concepts, interior design, and construction:
Imagineered Homes
Manasquan, NJ
www.imagineeredhomes.com
(732) 207-5009 & (732) 528-9206

Architecture:
Imagineered Homes and Harvest Homes

Furnishings:
Maine Cottage Furniture
www.mainecottage.com

Refined Comfort

Architecture:
Robert A. M. Stern and Gary Brewer
Robert A. M. Stern Architects, LLP
New York, NY
www.ramsa.com

Construction:
O. B. Laurent Construction
Santa Rosa Beach, FL
www.oblconstruction.com

Rentals:
Coordinated by Cottage Rental Agency
Seaside, FL
www.cottagerentalagency.com

A Touch of the South

Architecture:
Richard Gibbs, Architect
New Roads, LA

Rentals:
Coordinated by Cottage Rental Agency
Seaside, FL
www.cottagerentalagency.com